READY TO RIGHTSIZE?

A STEP-BY-STEP GUIDE TO YOUR RIGHTSIZING JOURNEY: FOR OLDER ADULTS AND THEIR LOVED ONES

JEANNINE BRYANT

Requests should be submitted to author directly at
Info@EasyRightsizing.com

Special thanks to:
Editor Kelsey Haugen
Cover Designer Ashley Erks

Get more rightsizing tips, information and inspiration at www.EasyRightsizing.com

Rightsize: *verb.* Convert (something) to an appropriate or optimum size.[1]

Or, more simply:

To find the perfect place between "too much" and "too little."

[1] "rightsize." *Merriam-Webster.com*. Merriam-Webster, 2019. Web. 3 Jan. 2019.

TABLE OF CONTENTS

Are you ready to rightsize?

Are you rightsizing? If so, you don't have time to read a big long book; you've got a mountain of work ahead of you! So, I'm going to keep this book, and the advice in it, short and to the point. This book is for anyone who is moving to a smaller home (downsizing) and needs to let go of a large percentage of stuff. It is also a book for loved ones of someone that is downsizing Or, for someone who simply has TOO MUCH STUFF.

Rightsizing is the process of finding the perfect place between "too much" and "too little." The majority of those who undergo the rightsizing process are older adults who have lived in their homes for a long time—decades—and now find themselves in a home that no longer fits. Are you living in a house that is too big for your needs with rooms that never get used? Are you living amongst piles and boxes of items you don't need, use, or love? If so, you need to rightsize. Are you ready?

This book is meant to be part playbook, part pep talk, and part kick in the pants to get going! Because, as the great de-cluttering expert Marie Kondo instructs, "Finish putting your things in order as soon as you can so that you can spend the rest of your life surrounded by the people and things that you love most."[2] Let's get through this rightsizing process so that you can get on with living a fantastic life!

I have worked as a senior move manager for nearly a decade. My company, Changing Spaces SRS, has a team of more than 20 individuals who work tirelessly to help our clients through the journey of letting go of a number of their items during the moving process. We believe in rightsizing: finding that perfect balance between too much house, too much stuff and having "just enough" to be happy,

---

[2] Kondo, Marie. *Spark Joy: An Illustrated Master Class on the Art of Organizing and Tidying Up*. Ten Speed Press, 2016.

healthy, and comfortable. We are experts in helping older adults sort through their belongings, plan for their new space, and navigate this time of transition effectively. Over the years, we have helped hundreds of older adults rightsize and move in our home city of Lincoln, Nebraska.

Often, when people are thinking about making a major life change, one of the biggest factors causing reluctance in moving is their STUFF. How ridiculous! Don't let pots and pans, clothing, décor, holiday items, books, electronics, tools, furniture, and whatever else is in your house (your STUFF) rule your life and decisions in such a way!

Do you need to rightsize? Ask if any of the following ring true:

- ✓ There are several unidentified boxes sitting in your basement, garage, or attic.
- ✓ You have clothing hanging in your closet that you haven't worn since Ronald Reagan was president.
- ✓ You are still holding on to gifts your friends or family members gave you simply because you'd feel too guilty to get rid of them.
- ✓ If asked where your birth certificate, passport, or marriage license are, you'd have no idea.
- ✓ There are boxes that are neatly packed, sealed, and stacked in a pile…from the last time you moved (which was several years ago).
- ✓ You have boxes and boxes of your children's items (toys, yearbooks, keepsakes, stuffed animals) …but your children aren't children anymore. In fact, they're grown up and have a home and family of their own.
- ✓ You've owned books for more than five years but never read them, have craft projects that have been "in process" (or never even started) for more than five years, or clothing that hasn't fit you in five years.

- ✓ There are bottles of lotions and potions in your bathroom that were purchased before the turn of the century (that's the year 2000!).
- ✓ You have a collection of every greeting card anyone has given you over the past 10 (or more) years.
- ✓ Your garage is used for storing lots of things…except for your car.[3]
- ✓ You pay a monthly fee to store your excess stuff in a self-storage unit (an industry raking in $38 billion nationwide each year!).[4]

Do any of these examples sound familiar? If so, then chances are that you need to rightsize. Never fear—there's no shame in that. The fact of the matter is this: the majority of people living in the United States have way too much stuff. Stuff we aren't using and stuff we don't love. Stuff we are keeping for no logical reason. Shockingly, in one University of California, Los Angeles study on the number of possessions in the average American household, researchers counted at least 2,000 possessions in a mere three rooms of a home.[5] Here in the U.S., we all tend to have more space than needed; the average American house size has more than doubled since the 1950s.[6]

So, how do you begin? There's an easy way to spot clutter. It is everything after "enough."[7] You see, there are the basic things that

---

[3] Sullivan, Meg. "L.A. Families Burdened with Too Much Stuff." *UCLA Newsroom,* 20 Mar. 2007, newsroom.ucla.edu/stories/garage-clutter. Accessed 10 Jan. 2019.

[4] Harris, Alexander. "U.S. Self-Storage Industry Statistics." *SpareFoot,* 19 Dec. 2018, sparefoot.com/self-storage/news/1432-self-storage-industry-statistics/. Accessed 10 Jan. 2019.

[5] Tuttle, Brad. "Got Stuff? Typical American Home Is Cluttered with Possessions – and Stressing Us Out." *Time,* 19 July 2012, business.time.com/2012/07/19/got-stuff-typical-american-home-cluttered-with-possessions-and-stressing-us-out/. Accessed 11 Jan. 2019.

[6] Adler, Margot. "Behind the Ever-Expanding American Dream House." *NPR,* 4 July 2006, npr.org/templates/story/story.php?storyId=5525283. Accessed 11 Jan. 2019.

[7] Robin, Vicki, and Joseph R. Dominguez. *Your Money or Your Life: 9 Steps to Transforming Your Relationship with Money and Achieving Financial Independence.* Penguin Books, 2018.

everyone NEEDS: clothing, blankets, dishes, towels. Then, there are the items that are nice little luxuries that make life more fun and comfortable: your favorite perfume, stylish clothing that make you feel great, tools and supplies that allow you to pursue a hobby. This is the point of "enough." Everything beyond "enough" is clutter—items you don't NEED (the essentials), and items you don't really WANT or USE (the luxuries). Clothing that doesn't look good on you or is never worn, tools that are never used, décor that doesn't make your house beautiful, toys the kids don't play with. This is the clutter that is impeding your life.

As I said before, you've got a mountain of work ahead of you, so this book will be short, to the point, and include lots of actionable steps that you can put into practice to make your downsizing journey easier. Now, let's get going!

Why? What's the rush? The reason is simply this: it's only going to get harder! Think you can't possibly move because of all the clutter in your basement? Or you just can't face the pile of stuff sitting in your garage? Guess what? The brutal reality is that sorting through all that stuff is only going to get harder. In one year, or two years, or five years, there will be more to sort through, and you'll have less energy to do it. Rightsizing looks different for everyone—sometimes it involves moving, sometimes it doesn't. But, it always involves sorting through your stuff. So, get started today with the rightsizing process, and begin living your best life now!

CHAPTER 1

PLANNING AND GETTING INTO THE RIGHT FRAME OF MIND

"There is a time for everything,
and a season for every activity under the heavens:
a time to be born and a time to die,
a time to plant and a time to uproot…
a time to keep and a time to throw away."
-Ecclesiastes 3:1-2, 6

FIRST: TIPS FOR PRESERVING MEMORIES

Before the first box is packed, take some time to capture some memories of your beloved home, just as it is. First, walk through the home with a video camera and take a tour of each room. Maybe you have a child or grandchild who could do this for you so that you can be in the video yourself, telling stories about special times or places in the home.

This may seem a bit silly, but just stop and think for a minute—wouldn't you LOVE to have such a video featuring your grandparents, giving a tour of their home? Wouldn't you love to see their kitchen, their bedrooms, their art on the wall? Trust me, a video like this will be a tremendous keepsake for your children and grandchildren!

Another idea is to simply take photos of your home—each room, just the way it is. Don't feel the need to clean up first; sometimes the best memories come from the items you just have laying around. It will help you to remember what it was really like to be in the home. I know when I'm looking at old photos of my grandparents' houses, I love seeing dishes on the counter, the toys on the floor (left by my brother and I), and the coat hanging on the back of a chair. I love it because it reminds me of all those little details of what it felt like to be in their home.

Finally, have one last big family celebration in the home before you move or make other major changes. Invite over as many friends and family members as you can. It needn't be a fancy event if you don't wish it to be. Simply ordering pizza and eating from paper plates is fine so long as the people you love are gathered together. This celebration is a great time to talk about the items you will be keeping after your move and the items you will be leaving behind. Perhaps you'll discover that friends or family would love to have an object or two from the home, and now is the best time to pass those things along to them!

GETTING INTO THE RIGHT FRAME OF MIND

Reframing is a powerful tool in all areas of life. It is the technique of looking at a situation in another way in order to change its meaning. I especially value reframing when working with older adults because, unfortunately, our society has historically held negative stereotypes about aging and subsequent residential transitions;[8] instead, these changes should be positive and full of growth! Reframing such concepts into positive language can help assign a more positive meaning to them. For example, you can view this transition as a negative one. *It's hard, change is scary, I'm nearing the end of my life, I like my stuff, and I don't want to give it up.* Or, you can view it as a positive change. *It's exciting, a new challenge, another chapter, a chance to reimagine my reality, a chance to pass along my possessions to bless others.*

---

[8] Fick, Donna M, and Nancy E Lundebjerg. "When It Comes to Older Adults, Language Matters." *Healio*, SLACK Incorporated, 28 Aug. 2017, healio.com/nursing/journals/jgn/2017-8-43-9/{94c64dd5-320b-4ccc-8993-2b3734e9b89d}/when-it-comes-to-older-adults-language-matters. Accessed 12 Jan. 2019.

Find a purpose for your rightsizing. Who are you doing this for? Yourself (so you can have less stress and take better care of yourself)? Your spouse (so they can get the care they need, or not feel the weight of all the excess stuff on their shoulders)? Your kids (so they are not burdened by all your stuff after you are gone)?

A practical tip for getting your mind right is to develop some positive mantras, or mottos, to live by throughout your rightsizing journey. Post them on your refrigerator. Write them in a journal. Repeat them daily. Do whatever you have to do to get yourself into the right frame of mind so that you can move through this transition with as much ease and grace as you can muster.

Examples might be:

- ✓ I'm going to prioritize PEOPLE over STUFF.
- ✓ You can't begin a new chapter if you keep rereading the last one.
- ✓ It's just stuff. STUFF and PEOPLE and MEMORIES are not the same thing. Stuff is just stuff. It can't replace people or memories or love.
- ✓ Things don't hold memories, people do. Just because I let go of an item doesn't mean I let go of the memory of the person, time, or place that it reminds me of.
- ✓ I can bless someone else with my excess. Letting go of all the "extras" in my house can actually be a blessing to someone else in my community.
- ✓ The most important things in my life aren't STUFF. It's my health, my relationships, and my experiences.
- ✓ Just because my children/grandchildren don't want my stuff, it doesn't mean they don't love me. STUFF and LOVE are not the same thing.
- ✓ The hearse doesn't come with a trailer. When my time comes, I can't take it with me!

By suggesting this way of reframing the process of letting go of your things, I don't mean to downplay the importance of STUFF in all of our lives. It's true that stuff shouldn't rule our lives, but our stuff really does contribute to our sense of self and identity. It's hard to let go of our stuff. If it were easy, you wouldn't be reading a book that coaches you through the process.

But, if it's true that your stuff is part of your identity, please know that you may have to reimagine yourself a bit. Realize that you are still YOU without your stuff. If you were to lose all your stuff, who would you be? Think about that for a minute—really. If a flood or fire or tornado hit and you lost all your stuff, who would you be? You would still be you. I encourage you to sit and think about that for a while. If you were to make a list of priorities in your life, they wouldn't be things, right?

Stuff requires time, money, and energy. Is your STUFF keeping you from what (or who) is most important? When you release that stuff, you can spend more time, money, and energy on your marriage, friendships, kids/grandkids, continuing education, experiences, volunteering, spirituality, health and wellness—the things in life that truly matter most.

One of my favorite terms for "getting rid" of stuff is "releasing." A recent client used this term when talking about the items that would not be making the journey with her to her next home, and I latched onto it immediately. Releasing your items has a feeling of liberation behind it—liberating yourself from the burden of too much stuff and liberating your "stuff" to be useful and have a new life out there in the world with another person who can put it to better use.

When facing an object that you know you don't really need, use, or love, ask yourself: How can this item be a blessing to someone else? Maybe it's a warm coat or a good novel that you no longer have a need for. Think of what a blessing it could be to someone who could really use a warm coat or a good book. The same goes for kitchen items; there are things sitting unused and unappreciated in your cupboards that someone else might be ecstatic to have. Ask friends and family members if they have any use for these items, or simply bring those items to a local charity where you know they will be put to good use. One person's clutter is another person's treasure. That old desk in your basement might be treasured to a student setting up an apartment. The barely used bed in the guest room could be an answer to prayer by refugees who have recently relocated to your city. Use your excess to bless others around you.

Another way to think about it is this: How will I use the extra space, time, or money that I will have after I release these items? Maybe you are paying monthly rent on a storage unit. According to 2018 self-storage statistics, nearly 10% of U.S. households rent a storage unit, which costs roughly $90 per month on average.[9] If you are one of them, think of all the money you will free up each month to use in a different way. How will you use that money? That could be a great motivator to release all the STUFF you've been paying to store.

Another way this applies is for anyone who has entire rooms of their homes dedicated to the storage of STUFF. If you cleaned out those rooms, what could you do with that space? Maybe turn it into a library? A craft room? A yoga studio or a meditation space? Think of the square footage you are giving up in your own home just to store STUFF that you aren't really using or loving. In fact, once you let go of the clutter in your home, you might find that a smaller home will suit you just fine!

---

[9] Harris, Alexander. "U.S. Self-Storage Industry Statistics." *SpareFoot*, 19 Dec. 2018, sparefoot.com/self-storage/news/1432-self-storage-industry-statistics/. Accessed 10 Jan. 2019.

Releasing items will also give you back time you spent sorting through, caring for, and cleaning those items. And, who among us couldn't use a bit more time?

ALLOW YOURSELF AS MUCH TIME AS POSSIBLE

"My house sold! I've got to be out in 30 days! What do I do now?!"

-A stressed client, who didn't adequately prepare

The most stressful situations are those in which someone is trying to rightsize against a hard deadline. Their apartment is ready at a retirement community and they start paying rent the first of the month, or their house has sold and is closing in four weeks.

Let me be clear: emptying out a house under a tight deadline is hard and stressful—I know because I've seen it time and time again. As a senior move manager, I've helped hundreds of clients who put themselves in a position to be under a short deadline. So, my advice? If you can avoid it, DON'T put yourself into a tight timeframe!

If it is feasible, the simplest approach to making the transition is to: find your new home , put a plan in place to pack and move into your new home, then sell and donate what remains in the house until it is empty, and THEN put the house on the market. Of course, some people need the money from selling their old house before they can move on to the next home. This is understandable, but you should know that it does add more stress to an already difficult situation. Getting a bridge loan from your local bank is a tool that is designed specifically for situations like this, and it makes the transition much easier.

Putting your house on the market before you have a new home to move into, or a plan in place to empty out the home, is always a risky venture. More often than not, it leads to a lot of unwanted stress in the weeks before closing.

CHAPTER 2
FACING YOUR FIRST MOVE IN DECADES

When you move, you must touch every single object in your home. It causes you to think twice about whether you want it or not. It's also a whole lot of work. This chapter will give you practical tips that you can implement to make your rightsizing process easier.

GO ON A TOUR OF YOUR HOME—DISCOVER WHAT'S ACTUALLY THERE!

It is shocking what you can find in your home if you actually look. The first step I recommend is simply to take a tour of your home—every room, every closet, every cupboard, and every drawer. Do you even know what you have? Many people do not. I hear time and time again from clients that my team is working with: "I don't even know what's in this [closet/cupboard/room]." To make it easier, be systematic about it. Start at the top floor of your home. Pick one room and look everywhere—top to bottom, left to right. Don't worry about de-cluttering anything just yet or making any decisions. Right now, you are simply on a discovery mission to note all the objects that are actually in your home.

Work your way around the room completely, opening each drawer and closet and cupboard. Then, move on to the next room and the next. Once that is done, move down to the next floor. If you have a two- or three-story house, start on the top floor, make your way down to the main floor, and finish with the basement. If you have objects in the attic, start there. And, don't forget the garage and the garden shed out back.

What this exercise will teach you is just how much STUFF you have in your home, and you will also discover places where you have multiples of items. Extra kitchen supplies that are stored in the basement are one example. Or, maybe you have postage stamps in three different areas of your home. Or a closet filled with coats on one level of your home and more coats stored away in the cedar closet downstairs. The goal is to take an inventory and discover what you have and what you've forgotten about completely.

THE LOGISTICS OF GIVING UP 50% OF YOUR STUFF

You may be leaving your family home where you raised your children, created lifelong memories, and spent the majority of your life. You may be downsizing the square footage of your home, moving from a house to a townhome or retirement community. This means you may have half (or less) of the square footage that you are used to. And, guess what that means? You've got to start making some hard decisions. What stays? And, what goes?

When you're giving up half (or more) of your possessions, the goal is this: Make sure the half you get to keep is your FAVORITE HALF. We are looking to discard the stuff that doesn't matter so that we can keep and treasure the stuff that does.

The first step is to start with furniture. Make a floorplan of your new space and start plugging in the pieces of furniture that meet the following criteria: they are functional, they fit the space, and you love them. Don't just eyeball this process—MEASURE! Measure the rooms of your new home and measure the furniture you are planning to move. Only then will you know precisely what will fit and what won't.

Next, move on to the small things that can be measured: books, clothing, and kitchenware.

- ✓ Measure the bookshelves you'll have in your new space—literally, get out the tape measure and note how many linear feet of storage you'll have for books. That tells you exactly how many books you can bring to your new home. Measure how much room you have currently to understand the difference and just how much downsizing is needed. Remember that we all have just two kinds of books in our house—those we have read and those we have not read. For those books you've already read, ask yourself how likely it is that you will reread them. If unlikely, it's an easy decision to let go of these books. For the books you have not yet read, ask yourself (truly) how likely you are to read them in the future. If the answer is not likely, then release them out into the world where someone else can read them, and they will no longer be taking up room on your shelves.

- ✓ Do the same with your closet. Measure the hanging space you've got in your new place and take only as many clothes as will fit in that space. A useful tip is to limit the number of hangers you have. Have only as many hangers as will comfortably fit in your hanging space, and vow to never buy another hanger for the rest of your life. That way, if you bring in a new item of clothing and have no free hangers on which to hang it, that signals you to go through and get rid of another item (or items). Consider, too, how many outfits you truly need. Today, the average American woman owns 30 outfits (one for every day of the month); in 1930, the average was only nine outfits.[10]

- ✓ Kitchen cupboards? Simple. Count how many cupboards you have in the new space and how many you currently have. Whatever the difference is shows you how much you've got to let go of. Let go of items that are rarely used; leave behind

---

10 Johnson, Emma. "The Real Cost of Your Shopping Habits." *Forbes Magazine,* 15 Jan. 2015, forbes.com/sites/emmajohnson/2015/01/15/the-real-cost-of-your-shopping-habits/#210eaee61452. Accessed 9 Jan. 2019.

multiples of items; and limit the number of dishes, glassware, and coffee mugs you bring (no need to bring a place setting for 18 if you won't be hosting large dinner parties).

The rest of your space can be filled in with décor, art, and other objects that bring you the most joy and/or serve a specific function. No more room for the "obligation items." Don't keep it just because your mother's cousin's daughter gave it to you. Keep it only if you LOVE IT.

THE POWER OF COUNTING

One of the best ways to keep yourself focused and grounded throughout the rightsizing process is to institute the *power of counting*. How many sets of sheets is appropriate to keep in your home? My answer is two sets for every bed in the house. One to wash and one to have on the bed. So, start by counting the beds in your home. Got three beds? Then, all you need is six sets of sheets. Just one bed being moved to your new home? Easy. Two sets of sheets should be moved with you. Pretty simple, right? Get rid of the rest.

Now, let's move on to towels. How many bath towels and washcloths do you really need in your home? You'll have to answer this one for yourself, but for my family and me, five towels and five washcloths per person in our house is plenty. There are four people in my house and, based on the number of times we bathe per week, the number of times we reuse a towel, and how often we do laundry, five is more than enough. Get rid of the rest!

In the kitchen, how many sets of measuring spoons and cups do you need? No more than two. What about spatulas or wooden spoons? Three of each should suffice, I would say. How many wine glasses do you have? And, how many times have you had that number of people at your home drinking wine all at once? What about coffee mugs?

Moving into your closet, I want you to count the pairs of jeans you have. Now, count how many sweaters you have. What about the number of black pants you own? This sort of exercise puts it all into perspective, doesn't it?

The power of counting is simple but very effective because it makes us face the facts and deal with the reality of how much STUFF we have. In our modern consumer society, mass acquisition of material goods is the dominant lifestyle.[11] You may have 35 coffee mugs hanging out in the cupboard or 45 pairs of socks shoved in a drawer or 20 pairs of jeans. So, start counting and put the amount of STUFF you are keeping into perspective. I dare you! You can download a free copy of my Power of Counting worksheet at www.EasyRightsizing.com.

A recent study found that throughout one's lifetime, a person will spend a total of 3,680 hours (or 153 days) searching for misplaced items, especially phones, keys, sunglasses, and paperwork.[12] In her book *The Life-Changing Magic of Tidying Up: The Japanese Art of Decluttering and Organizing,* Kondo offers valuable tips for tidying up your home and getting rid of the excess stuff that tends to accumulate.[13] One of the simplest and most helpful tips, I believe, is this: sort by category, not by room.

Give this a try with just a couple things and see what you think. Put all your bottles of lotion in one place. All your screwdrivers in one place. All your coffee mugs in one place. This opens your eyes to just how many duplicates you have of something. This applies to every kind

---

[11] Brown, Halina Szejnwald, and Philip J. Vergragt. "From Consumerism to Wellbeing: Toward a Cultural Transition?" *Journal of Cleaner Production*, vol. 132, 2015, pp. 1–10., doi:10.1016/j.jclepro.2015.04.107. Accessed 13 Jan. 2019.

[12] Daily Mail. "Lost Something Already Today? Misplaced Items Cost Us Ten Minutes a Day." *Associated Newspapers,* 20 Mar. 2012, dailymail.co.uk/news/article-2117987/Lost-today-Misplaced-items-cost-minutes-day.html. Accessed 11 Jan. 2019.

[13] Kondo, Marie. *The Life-Changing Magic of Tidying up: The Japanese Art of Decluttering and Organizing.* Ten Speed Press, 2014.

of possession you have in your home: towels, sheets, shoes, pants, sweaters, hammers, cleaning supplies, spatulas, magazines, electronics, toys, and more.

Don't neglect your refrigerator, freezer, or pantry, either. The power of counting applies to any groceries or paper goods that you've stockpiled in your home. Look at what you have and determine what you will reasonably eat/use up between now and when you intend to move and donate the excess. If items are expired, toss them out. You might be in the habit of keeping much more on hand than you actually cook anymore, and now is the time to start throwing out old food and distributing some of your excess, non-expired food and paper products to family and friends.

To stay on top of clutter on a continual basis, I suggest making a donation box a permanent fixture in your home. Put it in a closet somewhere so that it is both out of the way and easily accessible. This is now the place where you can always put an item you come across in your day-to-day life that you realize you don't need or want any longer. In placing items in the box, one at a time, you may be surprised at how quickly it fills up. Whether it's full once a week or once a month, this will become a signal to you to make a run to your local charity to drop off the items. This is a useful tool in controlling the amount of outflow in your home. Think about it—there is constantly an inflow of items to your home, but is the outflow keeping up in order to maintain a good balance of items in the home? Make combing through your items regularly a part of your lifestyle.

You can apply this same idea if you have items you wish to give to your kids or items you want them to look through before you let go of them. In this case, keep a box labeled for each of your children, and send it home with them the next time they come to visit! If they don't come to visit very often, you could package up the box and mail it to them when it's full. But, once you see the price of shipping, it might cause you and your grown children to reconsider whether keeping those items is worth the cost!

Don't wait! Things you can recycle or throw out this instant:

- ✓ Extra plastic containers and canning jars
- ✓ Magazines and catalogs (yes, even National Geographic)
- ✓ Expired medicines
- ✓ Your grocery bag collection
- ✓ Canned goods you won't eat
- ✓ Old paint cans
- ✓ Reader's Digest Condensed Books and encyclopedia sets
- ✓ Old electronics (TV, computer, radio, phone)

HIRING PROFESSIONALS TO WALK YOU THROUGH THE PROCESS

"If you think hiring a professional is expensive, try hiring an amateur."

-Julie Hall, The Estate Lady

Choose a senior move manager. This is my line of work, so, admittedly, I'm biased. But, it is my strongly held opinion that a senior move manager can make a transition so much easier and that they are worth their weight in gold. Senior move managers are specially trained and focused on helping their clients through a rightsizing transition from start to finish. They provide personalized, client-centered services and have the resources and expertise to help clients save money, lessen stress, and transition efficiently.[14] Most senior move managers can help you sort items, floor plan your new home, pack, manage move day, and unpack your belongings in your new home. All National Association of Senior Move Management (NASMM) members are educated and

---

[14] "About NASMM." *National Association of Senior Move Managers,* 2019, nasmm.org/about/index.cfm. Accessed 10 Jan. 2019.

trained, and they are held to strict legal and ethical standards. Visit NASMM.org to find a senior move manager near you.

Choose a mover. A list of local movers can be found in the Yellow Pages or by doing a quick search online. However, perhaps the best way to find a mover is to ask friends, family, and neighbors with whom they have had good experiences. Of course, only if you plan far enough in advance for your move do you have the luxury of being choosy. If you are scheduling a mover one or two weeks before your move during prime moving season, you might just have to take whoever is available—another reason to plan ahead!

Choose an estate liquidator. Estate liquidators are professionals who can empty your house quickly, while getting you some money for your things, by appraising, pricing, and selling your estate's entire contents.[15] There are many different business models; some liquidators organize and run tag sales or estate sales, others do auctions or online selling, and others may work with connections they have to individual buyers. The key point to remember is this: for a professional to agree to the work of liquidating the items in your house, there must be enough value in those items that taking a commission from the total sales allows the professional to make a profit. That means that if you don't have a lot of high-value items in your home, you might not be able to find an estate liquidator willing to work with you. In this case, the burden of selling what's left over falls on your shoulders.

Maybe you'll host your own garage or estate sale, maybe you'll work with local consignment shops, or maybe you'll donate a large portion of the items in your home to charity. Regardless, don't get too hung up on the price you get for the STUFF inside your home because your main asset is the house itself. The amount of money you get for

---

[15] "What is an Estate Liquidator?" *Estate Sales Blog*, EstateSales.org, 2019, estatesales.org/what-is-an-estate-liquidator. Accessed 10 Jan. 2019.

selling the STUFF inside your house is, by comparison, a small percentage of what you'll get for the home itself. I've seen far too many people become so focused on selling the stuff inside the house that it takes them several months (or even years) to empty it and put it on the market. They are focusing on the small dollar amounts and forgetting the major asset, quite literally being "penny-wise and pound foolish."

Choose a real estate agent. Your home is likely one of your largest assets, so choosing a real estate agent that will help sell it quickly, and for top dollar, is essential. As a starting point when looking for a realtor, you can go to online resources like Realtor.com and enter your zip code for a list of licensed real estate agents in your area (Realtor.com has more than 1 million agents nationwide).[16] Once again, recommendations from neighbors, family, and friends is perhaps one of the best ways to find good local options. It is common practice (and a good idea) to interview two or three real estate agents before choosing the one that you feel most comfortable with. Ask them to give you a market analysis of your home and ask about market trends in your city, neighborhood, and in homes within your price range. Ask them what suggestions they have for showing the home and any changes or repairs they believe would be a good investment. Ask them about their experience with selling homes in your area. Ask them how they would market the home. After you get all this information from a few different real estate agents, you'll have a good idea of who you believe is the right person for the job.

---

16 "Find a Realtor." *Realtor.com*, 2019, realtor.com/realestateagents. Accessed 13 Jan. 2019.

CHAPTER 3
NUTS AND BOLTS: PRACTICAL TIPS FOR RIGHTSIZING

There are five basic steps to any rightsizing journey. These steps are just a list of priorities that must be determined in order to rightsize your belongings efficiently. Make note of these five steps and conduct them IN ORDER if you want your rightsizing process to be as smooth as possible.

The first step in any rightsizing journey is to decide what you want to keep. Don't get distracted during this first step by wondering what you're going to do with the REST of the stuff in the house; for now, just focus on what you use regularly and what you love and absolutely MUST KEEP.

The second step is to decide what you will give to family and friends. This should be a combination of things you want to give to them and things they have asked for. Anything not going with you can be up for grabs. Maybe your children have a special memento or two from your home that they want for keepsake. Perhaps you have a grandchild or niece who is setting up their home or apartment for the first time and can put some of the extra bedding or kitchen items to good use. Remove this second layer of stuff next.

The third step is to determine which remaining items can be sold. How will you do this? Will you hire an estate liquidator to hold an estate sale or auction for you? Will you host your own garage sale? Will you sell items online (using sites like Craigslist, Facebook, or eBay)? Will you invite individual buyers or pickers (many times, these are antique dealers or re-sellers) into your home to make an offer on items? When selling your items and determining the amount of money you can expect to get from them, remember that supply and demand sets the price of everything (not your emotional attachment to it).

The fourth step is to donate what is left. Many charities provide free pickup of donations, but, often, items must be boxed and ready to go, located either on the curb or in your garage the day of the pickup. If you can't move the donation items yourself, you'll likely have to ask friends/family to help or pay movers to do the heavy lifting.

One of my pet peeves is a phrase I hear all too often: "This is just too nice to donate." Think about that statement for a moment. If something is "too nice" to donate, what is being implied? That we should only donate things that aren't nice? Do the people who benefit from our donations deserve nice things? Or, do they only deserve things that are worn out, outdated, slightly broken, or stained? Of course they should receive nice things! That's why the statement that it's "too nice" makes me cringe. The opportunity to bless someone with an excess item that they truly need and want is a wonderful one that should be taken advantage of whenever possible.

The fifth step of the rightsizing journey is to dispose of trash and recycling. Once again, this requires some hefty muscle to get the recycling and trash to the curb for pickup. If there is more trash than your local trash service will pick up, you might need to hire help. There are junk haulers located in many cities that can help you with this. Another piece to consider is any hazardous materials that can be found in your home (i.e., under the sink or out in the garage) that cannot be thrown out with your regular trash. Such materials include paint, pesticides, insecticides, oil, gas, and harsh cleaning and yard chemicals that have been long forgotten. Getting rid of these items takes a bit more planning and forethought. Each city or region has its own regulations for how these items must be properly disposed of. The best way to get accurate, local advice on how these items should be discarded can be found from your local health department. I would suggest searching online "hazardous waste" along with your city and state to locate the most up-to-date information and phone numbers to call.

After all five of these steps have been completed, the home will be empty and ready to be put on the market and sold. Going through these five steps to the rightsizing process in order is guaranteed to make the transition as smooth and seamless as possible. What happens, however, is that people often get mixed up in trying to focus on step 3 before they have finished with step 1. Or, they start discussing who gets what in step 2 while also determining what can be donated in step 4. Believe me, with my experience in helping hundreds of families through the rightsizing process and emptying out of a home, the process goes infinitely smoother if you follow these steps IN ORDER. By giving yourself these guidelines, it not only helps logistically keep things organized, but it gives you the mental clarity necessary to make good decisions about what to do with all the objects in your home.

The Five Steps to Any Rightsizing Project:

1. Decide what you want to keep
2. Decide what you will give to family and friends
3. Sell what you can
4. Donate the rest
5. Remove trash and recycling

WHEN IT'S HARD TO LET GO OF YOUR STUFF

I know that it can be very difficult for some people to let go of their belongings. We work with many people who grew up during the Great Depression or whose parents lived through it. No one likes to waste. Many were taught to "waste not, want not." But, if there are things sitting unused in your home that could be used by someone else, that IS wasteful. Keeping things that sit unused in your home is like stealing from the poor. Think for a moment of the items in your home you aren't using; are there less fortunate people in your community who could be putting that stuff to good use? You bet. The items in your home that you are keeping for "someday" are really needed today by someone in your community. Donate them!

Another reason it can be difficult to let go of something is because it was expensive. The sunk-cost fallacy explains why we tend to resist giving up items we paid a lot of money for. The sunk-cost fallacy is "a decision-making bias that reflects the tendency to invest more future resources [or time] in a situation in which a prior investment has been made, as compared with a similar situation in which a prior investment has not been made."[17] If you spent a lot of money on an object, you may think to yourself that you should keep it to avoid financial loss; or, if you get rid of it, you may think you should get some money out of it. But, here's the thing—you didn't initially put money into this item in hopes of getting something out of it. You bought it because you liked it, needed it, or wanted it. Now, you've owned it, enjoyed it, and used it. In letting it go, any money you are able to get out of it is a bonus, not a given. Through my work as a senior move manager, I have seen so many clients let this be a stumbling block for them in letting go of items they are no longer using.

Sorting through an entire house can be overwhelming and time-consuming, but let me share a trick that can make it go much faster: If there are certain rooms of your home (or entire levels of your home, like the basement or attic) that you rarely go into, chances are high that you don't need any of the objects in those rooms to come with you to your new home. Suddenly, your sorting job just got a whole lot easier! You hardly need to stick your head into those spaces when deciding what you'll keep because you already know that the

---

[17] Strough, Jonell, et al. "Are Older Adults Less Subject to the Sunk-Cost Fallacy Than Younger Adults?" *Psychological Science*, vol. 19, no. 7, 2008, pp. 650–652., doi:10.1111/j.1467-9280.2008.02138.x. Accessed 13 Jan. 2019.

likely answer is none of it! You aren't using it now, and you won't use it in your new place.

If you are having a hard time letting go of your items and want to keep more than will fit in your new space, you may be tempted to rent a storage unit for the excess stuff. Don't you DARE! If you aren't using the items now, you certainly are not going to use them when they are locked up in a shed across town. Do you know why most storage units take your credit/debit card information when you rent a unit? Because they put the monthly fee on an automatic debit so that you never have to think about it again. And then, guess what happens? You DON'T think about it again, and, before you know it, your stuff has been in storage for nine months (or two years, or 10 years) and you've not touched it. How much per month have you been paying? Do a little multiplication and figure out how much money you've lost storing stuff you don't need or use.

Hobby items that were a big part of your identity can also be difficult to give up. Maybe your hobby was golfing, quilting, woodworking, fishing, or painting. When was the last time you engaged in that hobby? Be honest with yourself. Just because you loved that hobby at one point in your life doesn't mean you must continue to keep all the stuff that goes along with that hobby if you haven't engaged in it during the last three years. If you do still engage in your hobby, find a way to keep only the items or tools essential to enjoying the activity.

Remember that the object of rightsizing is not to get rid of the things that you love—it is to prioritize your items and keep only your FAVORITE ones. Now is the time to set clear boundaries, define your priorities, and make decisions about what's most important to you. Remember that if everything is special, then nothing is.

ENLIST HELP

Start delegating! Set a date on the calendar, ask each kid and grandkid in your family to help you for one afternoon, and plan a specific task you'll accomplish during that time. If a holiday or family gathering is coming up soon, use that as an opportunity to tackle one closet, one room, or one stack of boxes when you have family members around you to help. Don't let them leave without taking a box or two with them!

And, on a similar note, now is the time to stop storing items for your grown children! Once your son or daughter reaches the age of 30 (or even 25), they should be responsible for storing any childhood items or memorabilia they wish to keep. Whether they have room in their own homes for these items or need to shell out money to rent a storage unit, that burden is one that should no longer be on the parents.[18] I've seen time and time again clients in their 60s or 70s who are still storing items that belong to their children, who are now grown and have homes of their own.

[18] Novack, Margit. "Stop Warehousing Your Kids' Stuff." *Moving Solutions*, 30 Sept. 2013, movingsolutions.com/2013/05/07/stop-warehousing-your-kids-stuff/. Accessed 14 Jan. 2019.

CHAPTER 4

HELPING A PARENT THROUGH THE RIGHTSIZING JOURNEY

"We all get organized eventually; we just might not be around for it."

-Sue DeRoos, professional organizer

I'm well aware that some readers who are drawn to this book may not be downsizing their own homes but, rather, downsizing the home of a loved one who is moving or has passed away. If your loved one is moving and the task of helping them through that transition has fallen to you, let me first applaud you. It is a lot of work, to be sure. This is a major undertaking, and the fact that you are doing it for a loved one is a testament to how much you care for that person. And, in case no one has said this to you recently, *THANK YOU.*

It's true what Sue DeRoos said, "We all get organized eventually; we just might not be around for it."[19] Sometimes, people get their own ducks in a row; other times, people have to do it for them. So many folks I've worked with have said, after having to downsize a loved one's home, "I'm not going to leave that burden to my children—I'm downsizing NOW!"

Through my experience as a senior move manager, my team and I are often privy to all kinds of family dynamics. We've seen the good, the bad, and the ugly—as well as the inspiring! We've seen some families struggle and fight through this transition and other families

---

[19] Doland, Erin. "What Will Be Your Legacy?" *Unclutterer*, 23 Aug. 2010, unclutterer.com/2010/08/23/what-will-be-your-legacy/. Accessed 10 Jan. 2019.

thrive and grow. My goal is to offer practical tips so that your family can be one that thrives through this process.

Focus on the PERSON, not on the STUFF

Take time to laugh and to cry throughout this process. Tell stories. Listen. Stop focusing so much on the stuff and focus on your loved one(s) and the huge life transition they are about to undertake. Talk to them about it. Also, pick your battles when it comes to the stuff involved in the transition. If your loved one isn't ready to give up that set of china, let them keep it for now. Even if they never end up using it in their new home, having one or two (or even five or six) boxes that stay packed away in a closet for the time being is not the end of the world. It's not worth a huge fight resulting in hurt feelings and resentments.

Many times, our relationship with our things is reflected in our relationships with other people. Truly, we have seen that for the people who have the healthiest relationships with their family and friends, their stuff doesn't matter all that much. Conversely, it is almost universally true that the family and friend relationships of hoarders are almost always strained. When you prioritize PEOPLE over STUFF, the result is positive. When you prioritize STUFF over PEOPLE, the result is negative.

Start Small and Start Early

Once again, the task of downsizing a loved one is so much easier if you are not under a time crunch. By starting early, you can eat the elephant one bite at a time, so to speak. If you are downsizing your parents' home and you have siblings, make it a rule that each time you or one of your siblings goes over to the house, they take one box or bag with them when they leave (whether it's trash, donation, or something you are taking to your own house).

And, let's stop right here and define the very first thing necessary to do if you are downsizing the home of a parent: Get out any of YOUR stuff that is still living in your parents' home! Whether it's keepsakes from your childhood or items from throughout your adulthood that you have "parked" there, the first step is to GET THAT STUFF OUT. As mentioned previously, it is no longer their job to store your stuff. And, you can't nag them about getting rid of their stuff if you haven't sorted through what is yours.

Secondly, talk to your loved one about which items they hope to give to family members and friends. If there are children or grandchildren or nieces or nephews who are at an age to set up their first home or apartment, now is a great time to let go of some of the practical furniture and household items left in the house. Beds, dressers, pots and pans, towels, sheets, and tools can all be put to good use and make your load lighter as you help your loved one downsize.

If your home, and your family members' homes, are already full, gently remind your parent that you only have room for the MOST IMPORTANT items because you already have a household full of stuff. In these situations, it is best to set a limit on how much you can take, such as one piece of furniture and three boxes of items, or whatever seems appropriate for the amount of space you have.

Your loved one may have strong opinions about an item or items "staying in the family," and, in situations like this, I remember a quote from author Gretchen Rubin: "Sometimes, we can be generous by taking."[20] If your loved one feels so strongly about something staying in the family and wants to give it to you, you can be generous by accepting that item, even if it's not something you feel strongly about. In fact, taking it doesn't mean you have to hold on to it forever. The simple act of accepting it in the first place makes a strong impact.

---

[20] Rubin, Gretchen. YouTube, 7 Jan. 2014, youtube.com/watch?time_continue=79&v=wmkRFiedBe4. Accessed 9 Jan. 2019.

The other side of that coin is that you must be able to let go of the guilt you feel for not keeping everything that belonged to your loved one. STUFF and MEMORIES and LOVE are not the same thing. When you are emptying out a home or drastically downsizing a loved one's belongings, keep nothing that makes you say, "I *should* keep that because it was Mom's" or "Grandma always had that in her dining room, so I *should* keep that" or "That's a family piece, so I *can't* get rid of that." Keep only objects that make you say, "I would love to have that." Anything else is being kept only out of obligation or guilt, which is not a good reason. Your loved ones would not want their things to be a burden; they would want them to be cherished. So, keep what you can cherish and let go of the rest. The items you let go of can be cherished by *someone else*—not necessarily you.

Sometimes there are items in the home that several people in the family would like to keep. I always say that this is a good problem; it means that an item is special and has enough positive memories attached to it that more than one person wants to cherish it in their home. But, here again, the idea is to prioritize PEOPLE over STUFF. Don't let the relationship suffer because of an object.

Make the process of dividing things up into a game. One idea is for everyone in the family to draw a card, and the highest number gets to choose one item first, then the next highest number, and so on. You can do round-robin until all the coveted items have been assigned. Another tactic that many families use is to involve immediate siblings only—no in-laws or children present. If you feel that would simplify things in your family, it's a good tactic to use. Perhaps the children get to pick the first round, and then grandchildren pick the second round. In-laws most likely have their own parents' STUFF to deal with, so they should have minimal input, in my opinion. We've seen families handle the division of items gracefully and peacefully, and we've seen families struggle and fight through the process. Rarely is the argument really about the STUFF. Most of the time, it's about an underlying relational issue that has been years in the making.

Tips for Making Your Loved One Feel at Home in the New Place

If you are moving your loved one to a new home, one way to assist them in completing an effective transition is to help the new place feel like home. Be sure to set up regular times to visit your loved one in their new space. Especially at first, this can be helpful as they are adjusting to a new environment and new routine. Encourage kids and grandkids to also visit often and to send mail—even care packages—to the new address.

Try to make the new space look as similar to their old one as possible by positioning their furniture in a way that is similar to the old house and hanging familiar art and photographs on the wall. Arrange the kitchen in a way similar to how it was arranged in the old house.

We all know that moving to a new place can feel lonely and intimidating at first, so surrounding yourself (or your loved one) with extra family support can help ease them through this adjustment period. Get a list of tips for helping your loved one adjust to their new home at www.EasyRightsizing.com.

CHAPTER 5
KEEP THE MEMORIES, NOT THE CLUTTER

One of the most difficult categories of stuff to get rid of is what we label "keepsakes." By definition, these are things that do not necessarily hold any functional value but that we keep merely for the sake of keeping them (thus, the term *keepsake*). It's important to identify these items in your home and understand that they serve no purpose to you other than sentimental (or obligation). What kinds of items fall into this category for you? Keepsakes can be anything: your great-grandmother's sewing machine, your great uncle's toolbox, your mother's fur coat. You don't really use any of these things, but you certainly can't get rid of them…or can you? Having some keepsakes, of course, is wonderful. Having boxes and boxes (or rooms upon rooms) full of keepsakes is not. In that case, the keepsakes become a burden instead of a blessing.

Here is the number one lesson I wish to pass on to you: Objects don't hold memories—people do! I personally love and appreciate family history. My father is a history buff and instilled in me, from an early age, the importance of remembering where I came from. I hope to instill the same value in my own children. But, does that mean I have to live in a museum? There comes a point when we need to make some hard choices and decide what to keep and what to let go of because we simply cannot keep it all. If we did, we'd have no room to live our lives in the here and now, making new memories.

Getting rid of the clutter doesn't have to mean we get rid of the memories. Here are some things to consider when making the determination of whether to keep an item that is attached to memories: First, ask yourself, what does this item remind me of? Is it a good memory? If it's not a good memory, the answer is easy—let it go!

There's no reason to hold on to things tied to negative emotions. If it is a good memory, I give you permission to keep it but ONLY if you can use it or display it somewhere in your home where you can recall that memory often. There's no use in keeping a good memory stored away in a box in the basement or attic!

Perhaps you have a piece of furniture in your home that does not serve a functional purpose, but it does serve an aesthetic purpose. I have my great-grandmother's spinning wheel, which I do not use to spin wool into yarn, but I do love how it looks. Therefore, its purpose is more than merely keepsake; it is aesthetic. However, another furniture item you might have is an old trunk stored away in your basement, garage, or attic. You no longer use it for a functional piece of furniture, and you don't appreciate the aesthetic of it (at least not enough to prominently display it inside one of the rooms in your home). So, why are you keeping it?

The second key to determining if a keepsake is truly worth keeping is to ask yourself why you feel compelled to keep it. Is it because it reminds you of someone you love? Because you would feel guilty getting rid of it? Because you don't know what else to do with it?

When working with memorabilia, professional organizer, blogger, and author Erin Rooney Doland has some good advice in her book *Never Too Busy to Cure Clutter*: "Since I can't keep everything, is this item the best example of the memory I wish to be keeping? … Am I keeping these things because they continue to bring me joy and serve as documents of my happiness? If I'm not holding on to these items because of their significance in my life, why am I holding on to them at all?"[21]

The third thing to consider: If I got rid of this item, would I forget the memory? The answer to this question is likely NO. Letting

---

[21] Doland, Erin Rooney. *Never Too Busy to Cure Clutter: Simplify Your Life One Minute at a Time*. William Morrow, an Imprint of Harper Collins Publishers, 2016.

go of an object doesn't mean you'll forget about that person or event if it was important to you. Challenge your thoughts on this subject—what would (really) happen if you no longer had your grandmother's antique vanity? Would you forget about her? Would the love you shared with her go away? Of course not. Remember: STUFF and MEMORIES and LOVE are not the same thing!

KEEP ONLY ITEMS THAT YOU WILL USE OR DISPLAY

Something else to consider might be: Is there another way to keep this memory alive? For instance, if you have a pump organ or piano that you don't play but keep because it used to belong to a family member, perhaps you could find a photo of your loved one playing the organ or piano. A nicely framed photograph, prominently displayed, would allow you to honor your loved one (and take up much less space than a huge, unused piano or organ). The biggest lesson I can offer here is to keep only the most meaningful objects that you can USE or DISPLAY.

I'm willing to bet that most of us have a box or two (or three or more!) of keepsake items that are stored away in a basement, attic, or another area of the house that you rarely see. The problem with these boxes, and the memories in them, is this: if these memories never see the light of day, then what good are they?

If you have items in your life that you are keeping because they are attached to memories, then that means those memories are important to you. They are worth remembering. So, it makes sense to want to see and recall those memories often. This isn't feasible when those keepsake items are stored away in a room you are rarely in, like the basement or attic.

My advice to you is to find practical ways to display or use the keepsake items in your life. One example might be to use an item in a decorative way. Put small objects in a shadow box that can be hung on a wall. Use heavy items as bookends on your bookshelves. Buy a beautiful tray or glass box to display keepsake jewelry on your bedroom dresser. Frame old recipes written by loved ones and hang them in your kitchen. These are just a few ideas to get you started.

The other option is to find a way to make the keepsake items useful. An antique teacup can be used to hold paperclips on your desk. The glassware and china that belonged to an ancestor can be used on a daily basis, not just stored away for special occasions. Wear the fur coat your grandmother left you. Use the tools you received from your great-uncle. Don't be afraid to let kids read the old childhood books you've kept or play with your old toys.

Every time you see these items, good memories of your loved ones will come flooding back, and that's the main reason we keep these items—to remember and honor them. I often think that my (long deceased) grandparents and great-grandparents would be thrilled to see some of their items in my home, being used by members of my family or displayed in a place of honor as things of beauty. They would know that they are remembered and cherished.

A selection of favorite items from loved ones that are used in meaningful ways is a whole lot better than a slew of objects packed away in dusty (or moldy) boxes.

PASSING ITEMS DOWN TO LOVED ONES

We often wish to pass down family heirlooms to our children and grandchildren, hoping that they will cherish these heirlooms as much as we do. When passing down an item to a loved one, tell them the story behind the item. Who was its original owner? When and where did they get it? How did you end up with it? What are the memories you associate with it? Often, the things your family will care about are those with a story—objects you (or past family members) have used and/or displayed at home, rather than things that have been in a box, untouched, for decades.

I can't tell you exactly what your kids will want to keep someday when you're gone, but I can tell you this: the answer will most likely surprise you. It's not always the items you wish they would keep—fine china, crystal goblets, fur coats, expensive collectibles, or antique furniture. This doesn't mean that your family doesn't love you or want to remember you when you are gone. Their memories of you may not be tied to these fancy items that only came out on special occasions once or twice a year.

Instead, an item of choice might be a silly one they remember from their childhood or one that is tied to a particular family tradition—even an inside joke. It might be something deeply personal that holds more meaning to them than an item of high monetary value.

My advice to clients encountering a situation in which family members aren't choosing to keep items they wish they would keep is this: just because the item is most meaningful to you doesn't mean it will be most meaningful to your children and grandchildren. Be assured, they will want to keep something! But, it might be something as simple as the sweater you used to wear around the house, the fishing poles they remember using with you on vacations as a child, a hymnal you used to sing from, or maybe just a box full of handwritten letters, notes, or recipes collected throughout the years.

Try not to worry too much about which items your family will choose to keep and treasure after you are gone. For now, forget about the stuff and focus on making memories together - because that is truly the best keepsake of all!

TACKLING THE PHOTOS

The first thing we need to agree on when tackling your boxes and boxes of family photos is that you don't need to keep every photo! That might seem shocking—I know—but it's true. As with any organizational project, we must first begin with discarding. That way, we are only faced with organizing that which we truly need or want to keep.

As you sort through your photos, ask yourself how meaningful they are. From that trip to Colorado you took in 1973, how many of those photos are keepers? The answer, of course, is likely just a few—and those that you choose to keep will probably be the ones with people in them. Scenery shots of mountains and trees are fun to take in the moment but rarely stand the test of time.

Another question to ask is: how many photos of a particular event do you need to keep? For that baby shower you hosted for your cousin 20 years ago, do you need to keep 50 photos of that occasion or will five suffice? What about photos you come across that have no emotional ties for you, such as photos of people you don't recognize or barely knew? Are you beginning to see my point? Not every photograph is worth keeping!

Examples of photos you can toss NOW:

1. Duplicates of the same photo (keep one and toss the rest or give them to other family members!)
2. Scenery photos with no people in them and no emotional tie for you
3. Photos of people you don't like (yes, really!)
4. Photos of you that you don't like (yes, really!)
5. Multiple photos from the same event (50 photos from one bridal shower, for instance, when 10 would suffice)

As for the photos you do keep, now is the time to label them! Write a short note on the back with an approximate date and the names of people in the photo. It needn't be a long description—just some basic information so that, someday, someone other than you will know who is in the photo and when it was taken.

Lastly, in order to truly protect your family's photos and memories, you must digitize the photos—and back up the files! Printed photographs can be digitized by scanning them onto your computer. This can be done in your home office with a desktop scanner, or you can send them off to a company to be scanned. A photo-scanning service like Legacy Box can turn this time-consuming task into a breeze, and it would be a fantastic gift for a loved one who is downsizing![22] Visit www.LegacyBox.com to learn more about the service.

Once those photos are on your computer, however, they aren't safe until that data has been backed up. There are many online companies that will automatically back up your data daily so that you can rest assured that your photos are safe for generations to come. My family uses www.Backblaze.com for affordable computer backups and cloud storage.[23]

When Someone Dies: Keeping Things That Once Belonged to a Loved One

When we lose someone we love, it's very common to want to hold on to them in any way we can. Usually, this manifests itself by way

[22] "Digitize Your Home Movies & Photos with Legacybox." *Legacybox*, 2019, legacybox.com. Accessed 10 Jan. 2019.

[23] "Backblaze Online Backup." *Online Backup Security & Encryption | Backblaze*, Backblaze, 2019, backblaze.com. Accessed 10 Jan. 2019.

of keeping their belongings. This is a normal and completely healthy thing to do in those first weeks and months of mourning a loved one.

However, when the time comes to begin to sort through these items that once belonged to your loved one, how do you decide what to keep and what to let go of? It is tempting, I know, to keep it all. Or, at the other extreme, some might be tempted to get rid of it all to forget in hopes of easing the pain. Like anything, the answer lies in the perfect middle.

Selecting a few meaningful objects that belonged to your loved one is the key to striking that happy balance between "too much" and "too little" when it comes to a deceased person's belongings. I bet we all know someone who has boxes of a deceased relative's items stored away in a basement or attic because family members aren't yet ready to sort through the objects or are burdened with guilt whenever they think of getting rid of them.

Ask yourself: would you remember your loved one better if you kept 50 of their items instead of 30? What about 20 of their items instead of 10? Do more objects equal more memories? The answer, of course, is no.

So, where do you draw that line? Everyone must come up with a limit that they feel comfortable with but make no mistake—some kind of limit should be set. It is extremely helpful to go ahead and actually COUNT the individual items you have that belonged to your loved one. You might be surprised at the number. We have found that some people are keeping literally HUNDREDS of items that they don't use or love just because they once belonged to someone who is no longer living.

Think about the person you are missing and the items that most remind you of them. Now, think about how you can incorporate those items into your everyday life, either on display or used in your home, so that you see and remember that person often. That helps winnow down the collection of items quickly.

I speak from experience. I lost my mother in 2005, and I know all too well that her stuff is not going to bring her back, and it's not going to help my family members or I remember her any more than we already do. Stuff is just stuff. Memories come from people and experiences, not from stuff. And, just because I choose not to keep every object that once belonged to my mother doesn't mean that her memory isn't important to me. Keeping a loved one's items doesn't bring them back. The memories we have of that person aren't tied to these objects, and they won't go away with the object itself. People hold memories; objects do not.

Get a free printable worksheet that will help you determine which items you'll keep and how they can be used at www.EasyRightsizing.com.

In Conclusion

Author Simon Sinek says, "The mind can be convinced, but the heart must be won."[24] There aren't many who can argue with the logic of rightsizing, of putting your possessions in order now rather than waiting until it's too late and leaving the burden to your loved ones. But, the same is true for eating our vegetables and exercising, right? We all know it's good for us but not everyone does it. Our minds may be convinced, but our hearts must be won if this information is to lead to action.

Rightsizing is about changing your attitude toward your STUFF and getting into a different frame of mind. It's about focusing on what matters most—our families, our friends, our experiences, our spirituality—and seeing our STUFF for what it is: *just stuff.* I hope that I have inspired you to hold on to only the most important objects in your life and let go of the rest. I hope that I have given you both the information and inspiration to get you Ready to Rightsize!

---

[24] Sinek, Simon. *Together Is Better: A Little Book of Inspiration*. Portfolio/Penguin, 2016.

About The Author

JEANNINE BRYANT is an expert at helping older adults and their loved ones through times of transition. As the owner of a senior move management company in Lincoln, Nebraska, she has helped hundreds of older adults through the rightsizing process, taking them by the hand and walking them through the transition from start to finish. Jeannine has a passion for helping others understand the benefits of rightsizing their homes and belongings. She lives in Lincoln with her husband and two children.

Get more rightsizing tips and information at www.EasyRightsizing.com

Learn more about Jeannine's Senior Move Management Company, Changing Spaces SRS, at www.ChangingSpacesSRS.com

A number of FREE companion resources are available at www.EasyRightsizing.com

*Clutter-Free Gift Ideas

*The Power of Counting Worksheet

*What to Keep When a Loved One Dies

*Tips to Make Your Loved One Feel at Home in Their New Space

…And many more videos, blog posts and tips offered about the rightsizing journey!

ONE LAST THING…

If you enjoyed this book or found it useful, I would be very grateful if you'd post a short review on Amazon. Your support really does make a difference, and I read all the reviews personally so that I can receive your feedback and make future books even better.

Thanks again for your support!

Made in the USA
Middletown, DE
21 September 2024